A FIREFLY BOOK

Published by Firefly Books Ltd. 2016

First printing

Publisher Cataloging-in-Publication Data (U.S.)

Names: Besson, Agnès, author. | Surein, Manuel, illustrator.
Title: My first 1000 animals / Agnès Besson ; illustrator Manuel Surein.
Description: Richmond Hill, Ontario, Canada : Firefly Books, 2016. | Originally published by Larousse, Paris, France, 2013 as Le Larousse des 1000 animaux. | Summary: A picture book for beginning readers. Covers words for animals based on their habitats: forest, jungle, and ocean.
Identifiers: ISBN 978-1-77085-796-4 (hardcover)
Subjects: LCSH: Animals — Juvenile literature. | Vocabulary – Juvenile literature. | Vocabulary – Pictorial works – Juvenile literature.
Classification: LCC PE1449.B477 | DDC 428.1 – dc23

Library and Archives Canada Cataloguing in Publication

A CIP record for this title is available from Library and Archives Canada

Published in the United States by
Firefly Books (U.S.) Inc.
P.O. Box 1338, Ellicott Station
Buffalo, New York 14205

Published in Canada by
Firefly Books Ltd.
50 Staples Avenue, Unit 1
Richmond Hill, Ontario L4B 0A7

Printed in China

Conceived, designed, and produced by
Larousse, 21 rue du Montparnasse – 75006 Paris

Publishing Director: Isabelle Jeuge-Maynart and Ghislaine Stora; Editorial directors: Stéphanie Junique and Florence Pierron-Boursot; Editor: Marie-Claude Avignon; Art director: Laurent Carré; Design: Sylvie Fécamp; Copyeditor: Anne Caneparo; Production: Rebecca Dubois; Translators: Claudine Mercereau and Nancy Foran

My First 1000 Animals

Agnès Besson
Illustrator: Manuel Surein

FIREFLY BOOKS

Contents

animals in their environment

Pets in the Home 8

In Parks and Gardens 10

In the Country 12

On the Farm 14

In the Woods and Forests 16

In Ponds and Rivers 18

In the Mountains 20

On the Seashore 22

In the Oceans 24

In the Savanna 26

In the Heart of the Rainforest 28

In Deserts 30

In Cold Regions 32

In the South Pacific 34

the lives of animals

Birth — 36

Baby Animals — 38

To Each His Home — 40

All Clean! — 42

Moving Around! — 43

Feeding! — 44

Attacking and Defending — 46

Communicating — 48

Sleepy Time! — 50

amazing animals

Animals from The Past — 52

Unbelievable Outfits — 54

Record-Setting Animals — 56

Extraordinary Animals — 58

Pets in the Home

wheel

guinea pig

cage

hamster

rabbit

ferret

mouse

petting

cat

dog bed

playing

litter box

cat

whiskers

kittens

claws

water bowl

eating

tail

fish

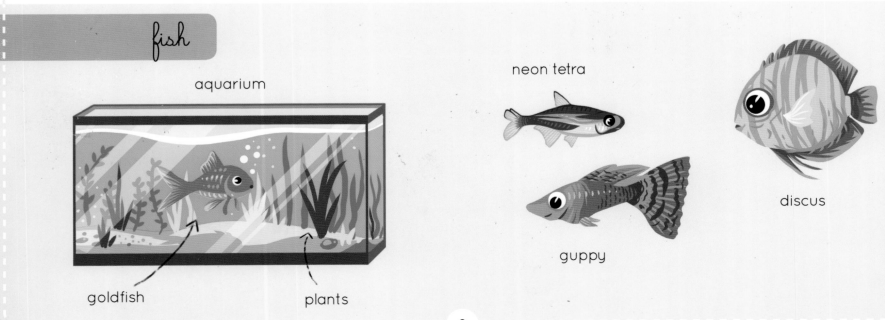

neon tetra

aquarium

discus

goldfish

plants

guppy

cockatoo

serin

budgie

birds

canary

birdcage

finch

ghouse

dog

muzzle

nose

dog

puppy

ball

turtle

shell

playing fetch

enclosure

popular dogs

German shepherd

Jack Russell

Chihuahua

Labrador retriever

9

In Parks and Gardens

wasp

fly

small tortoiseshell butterfly

bee

mosquito

firebug

gnat

wings

sparrow

beak

swans

hedge

garden dormouse

hedgehog

pond

two antennae

head

abdome

six legs

chest

ant

quills

rolling into a ball

small critters

spider

centipede

eight legs

black scorpion

web

claws

10

nuthatch

robin

wren

song thrush

great tit

wall lizard

ladybug

aphids

worm

snail

beetle

slug

blackbird

pigeon

magpie

peacock

In the Country

polecat

European hamster

weasel

hare

linnet

swallowtail butterfly

field mouse

dormouse

vole

praying mantis

golden ground beetle

mole

ermine

tunnels

ring-necked snake

chirping
cicada

crackling
locust

chirping
cricket

harvest
mouse

grasshopper

nest

quail

skylark

rabbits

burrow

buzzard

hawk

harrier

partridge

red
kite

13

On the Farm

snout

tail

boar

pig

sow

piglets

donkey

barn

bull

stab

milking

cow

calf

ox

horse

mare

colt

lamb

kid

ram

ewe

sheep

Billy goat

goat

rabbit hutch

doe

bunnies

nest

rabbits

pond

duck

chicken coop

eggs

ducklings

drake

comb

chicks

hen

rooster

strutting

goose

guinea fowl

turkey

gander

gobbler

In the Woods and Forest

wild boar

fox

badger

deer

oak tree

doe

antlers

sow

stag

mud wallow

fawn

wild boar piglets

acorns

poplar admiral butterfly

little creatures

red wood ant

stag beetle

woodlouse

millipede

jay

tawny owl

owl

turtle dove

cuckoo

dormouse

spotted woodpecker

bushy tail

green woodpecker

woodcock

squirrel

acorns

treetrunk

in the forest of North America

grizzly bear

lynx

porcupine

bison

wolverine

17

In Ponds and Rivers

toad

newt

water strider

water spider

heron

coypu

coot

lily pads

frog

tadpoles

gudgeon

dragonfly

damselfly

carp
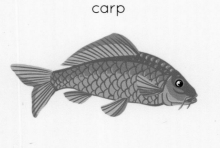

mayfly

mallard
duck

18

perch

pike

dipper

crayfish

muskrat

beaver dam

beaver

kingfisher

trout

otter

otter pups

spotted salamander

in the rivers and lakes of Africa

catfish

egret

pelican

Nile crocodile

In the Mountains

mouflon

marten

Eurasian lynx

wolf

brown bear

peregrine falcon

Eurasian eagle owl

chamois

mountain hare

short-tailed weasel

rock ptarmigan

groundhog

wood grouse

bearded vulture

golden eagle

talons

20

snow leopard

urial

yak

markhor

panda

in winter

chamois

snow vole

mountain hare

alpine chough

entrance to the burrow

ermine

rock ptarmigan

groundhog

in the Andes mountains

condor

chinchilla

vicuña

puma

guanaco

21

shell

sea urchin

clam

oyster

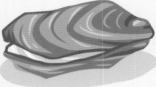

razor clam

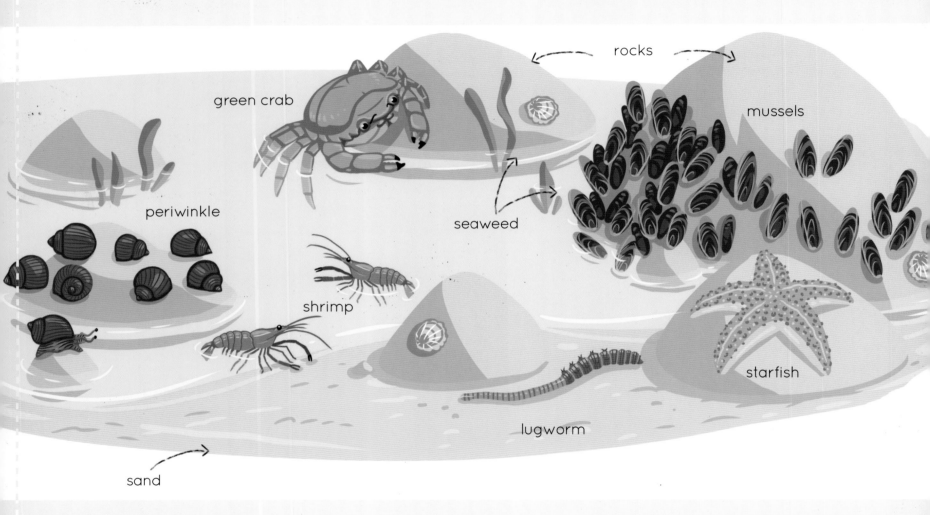

green crab

rocks

mussels

periwinkle

seaweed

shrimp

starfish

lugworm

sand

crab

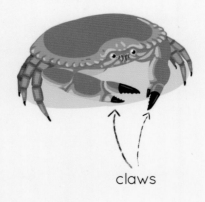

claws

spider crab

limpet

hermit crab

sea robin

mackerel

stingray

sole

fins

scales

sea bass

black-headed gull

northern gannet

seaweed nest

albatross

razorbill

murre

seagull

Atlantic puffin

cliff

tern

seagull chicks

In the Oceans

jellyfish

seahorse

sperm whale

great white shark

parrot fish

butterfly fish

sea turtle

lionfish

moray eel

sea anemone

clownfish

giant clam

coral

triggerfish

wildlife of the deep ocean

goblin shark

anglerfish

giant squid

pelican eel

frilled shark

blue whale

tuna

school of mackerel

gray reef shark

dolphins

dolphin calf

octopus

grouper

tentacles

suckers

crayfish

lobster

In the Savanna

antelopes

baobab

lioness

lion

rhinoceros

lion cubs

elephants

elephant calf

panther

hippopotamus

ibis

savanna monitor

stork

sulcata tortoise

ostrich

white-backed vulture

black-crowned crane

cormorant

pink flamingo

giraffe

gazelles

acacia

waterbuck

jackal

zebras

baboon

warthog

cheetah

buffalo

rock badger

wildebeest

hyena

In the Heart of the Rainforest

in the African jungle

chimpanzee

pangolin

gorilla

in Asia

orangutan

tiger

in the Americas

kinkajou

ocelot

giant anteater

jaguar

armadillo

tarantula

peccary

tapir

in rivers

poison-dart frog

piranha

harlequin poison frog

caiman

anaconda

vines

green vine snake

macaw

howler monkey

quetzal

hummingbird

spider
monkey

marmoset

macaw

sloth

emerald tree boa

toucan

In Deserts

family of meerkats

leopard
tortoise

pin-tailed
sandgrouse

springbok

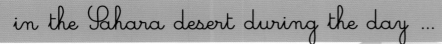

in the Sahara desert during the day ...

dunes

addax

white-crowned
wheatear

ariel gazelle

sand lizard

rock
badger

sand

fennec

dromedary camel

spiny-tailed
lizard

jerboa

sand viper

in rocky deserts of North America

roadrunner

great horned
owl

cougar

desert
hare

coyote

rattlesnake

addax

hyena

... and at night

fennec

wildcat

jerboa

horned desert viper

sand viper

dung beetles

scorpion

31

In Cold Regions

big and small animals...

the North Pole

... of the tundra

arctic fox

musk ox

reindeer

razorbill

polar bear

polar bear cubs

ivory gull

tusks

walrus

ice floe

beluga

whiskers

seal

narwhal

bowhead whale

snowy owl

arctic hare

lemming

moose

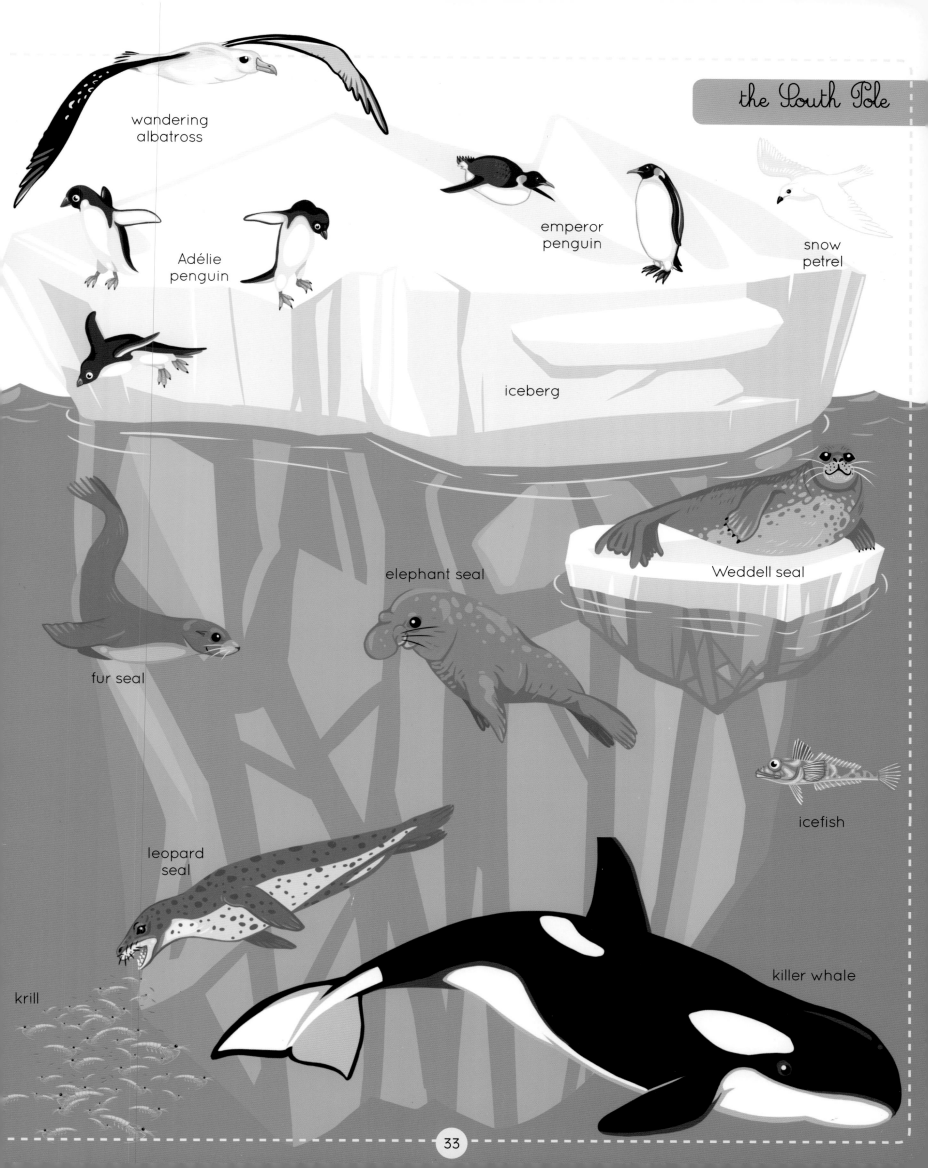

wandering albatross

Adélie penguin

emperor penguin

snow petrel

iceberg

Weddell seal

elephant seal

fur seal

icefish

leopard seal

killer whale

krill

33

In the South Pacific

platypus

saltwater crocodile

loggerhead sea turtle

dugong

kangaroo

dingo

emu and her little chicks

pouch

monitor lizard

bearded dragon

frilled-neck lizard

splendid wren

sulfur-crested cockatoo

southern cassowary

wedge-tailed eagle

cuscus

pig-nosed turtle

echidna

snake-necked turtle

eucalyptus

opossum

wallaby

koala

wombat

numbat

quoll

kiwi

blue bird of paradise

superb bird of paradise

crowned pigeon

Birth

in an egg

blue egg of
the blackbird

hen's
egg

crocodile
egg

big ostrich egg

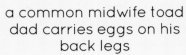 

a common midwife toad
dad carries eggs on his
back legs

emperor penguin
dads

ice floe

thick
plumage

emperor
penguin egg

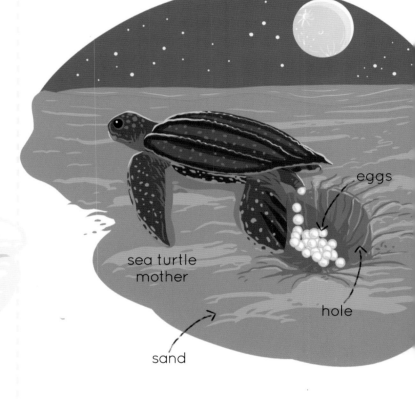

sea turtle
mother

eggs

hole

sand

the babies

chick

crocodile
hatchling

ostrich
chick

broken egg

sea turtle
hatchlings

whale calf

whale mother

a mother bat gives birth upside down

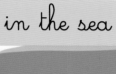
in the sea

a killer whale calf is pushed toward the surface

mother killer whale

on land

giraffe mother

a baby giraffe falls from a great height

dolphin calf

baby seahorses

seahorse father

dolphin mother

ventral pouch

dolphin "godmother"

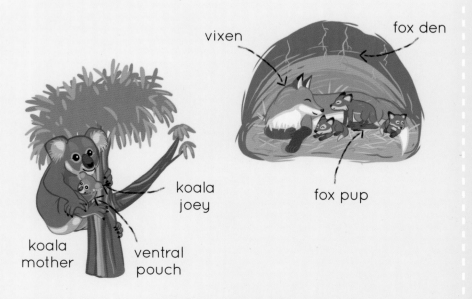
vixen

fox den

koala joey

fox pup

koala mother

ventral pouch

Baby Animals

well-protected babies

feeding

chick

kingfisher

hippopotamus mother

suckling underwater

hippopotamus calf

baby gorilla

gorilla mother

washing

prairie dog mother

prairie dog pup

adult emperor penguin

emperor penguin chicks

nursery

elephant mother

elephant

elephant calf

learning

mother bear

salmon

a brown bear cub learns how to fish

otter

a tiger cub learns to hunt

tiger mother

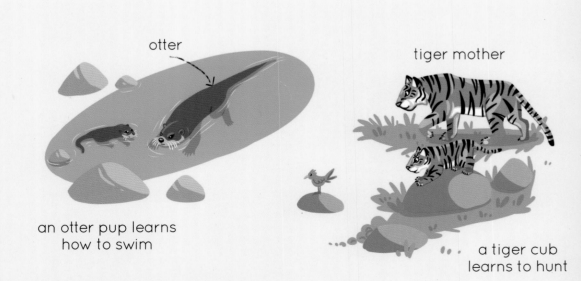

an otter pup learns how to swim

koala joey

scorpion babies

funny baby carriers!

on the back

ring-tailed lemur baby

possum babies

in the mouth

lioness

the scruff of the neck

young crocodile

lion cub

on the rump

baboon baby

wombat joey

in a pouch

kangaroo joey

in the arms

orangutan baby

on the belly

sloth baby

in the wings

swan cygnet

on the feet

penguin hatchling

To Each His Home

underground

entrance to a burrow

burrow

badger

underground village

prairie dogs

rooms

tunnels

natural shelters

shell

snail

empty shell

hermit crab

shell

turtle

giant clam

amazing nests

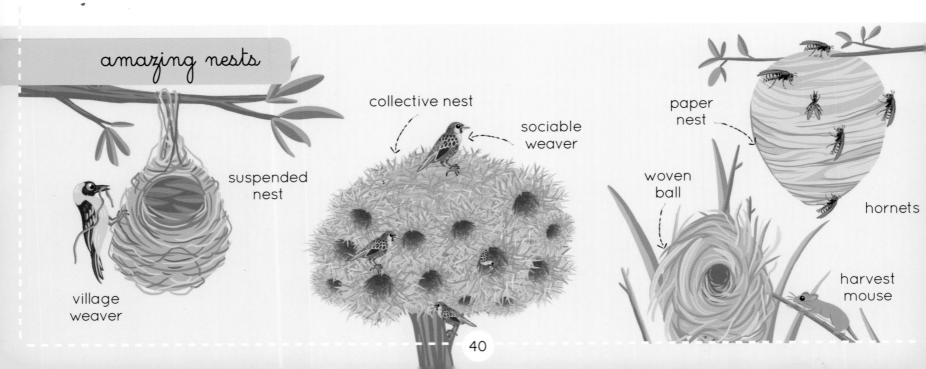

collective nest

sociable weaver

paper nest

suspended nest

woven ball

hornets

village weaver

harvest mouse

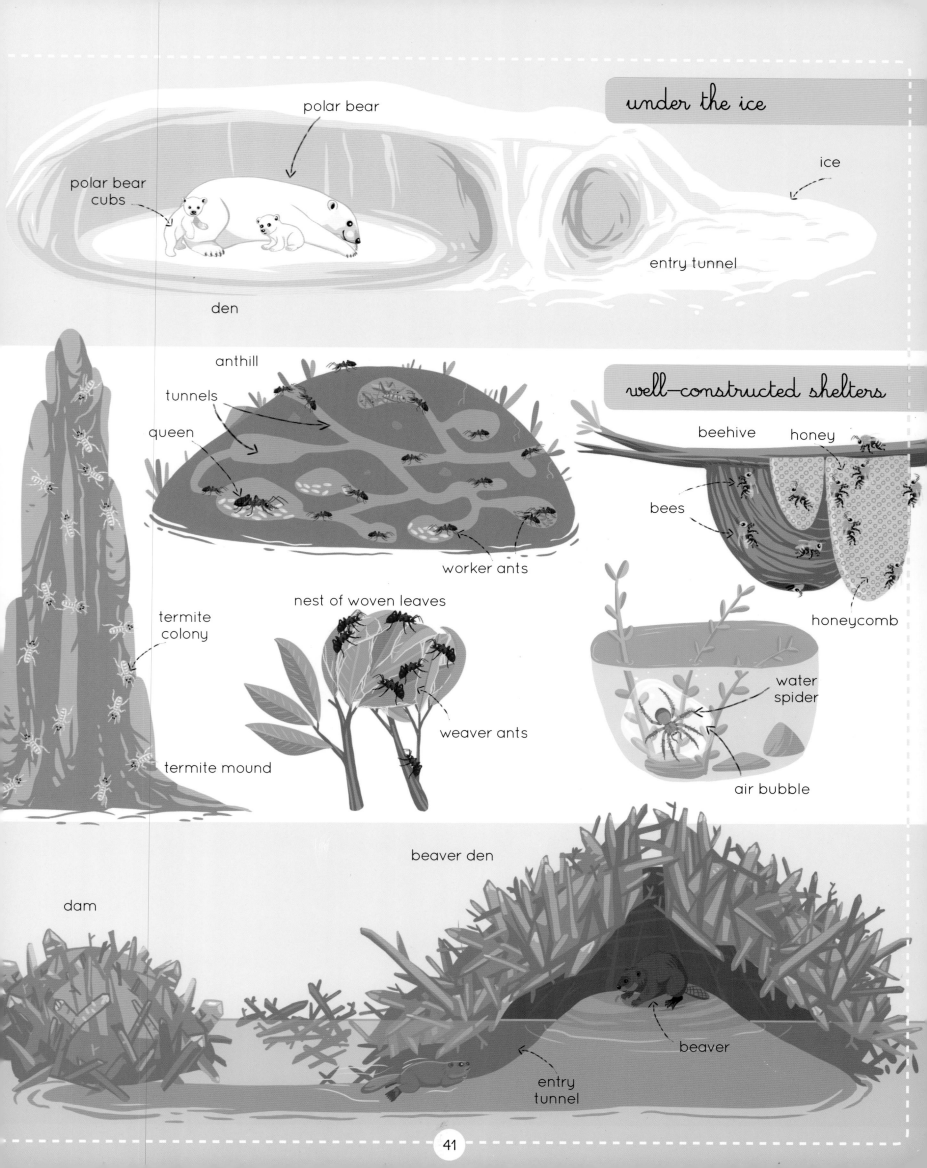

polar bear

polar bear
cubs

ice

entry tunnel

den

anthill

tunnels

queen

well-constructed shelters

beehive

honey

bees

worker ants

honeycomb

termite
colony

nest of woven leaves

weaver ants

water
spider

termite mound

air bubble

beaver den

dam

beaver

entry
tunnel

All Clean!

a robin washes itself
in a puddle

a goldfinch
smoothing its feathers

a sparrow takes
a dust bath

a cormorant dries its
feathers in the sun

a blue jay takes
an ant bath

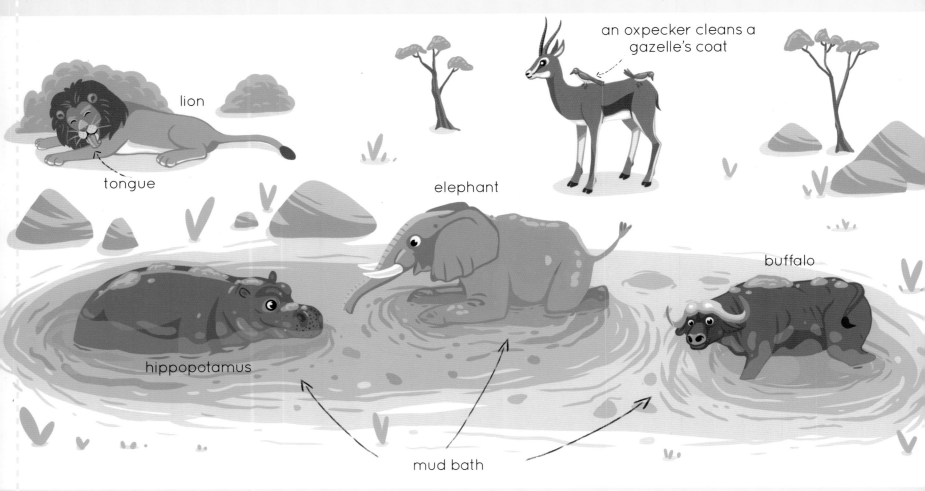

lion

tongue

elephant

an oxpecker cleans a
gazelle's coat

buffalo

hippopotamus

mud bath

help with grooming

vervet monkeys
delousing each other

a plover cleans
a crocodile's teeth

a mongoose cleans a
warthog's coat

a bluestreak cleaner
wrasse cleaning a
moray eel's teeth

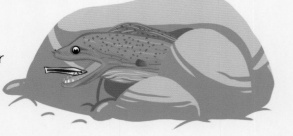

an albatross glides

a hummingbird flies
in place

flying dragons glide
from tree to tree

a swallow flies by
beating its wings

a horse gallops

a penguin slides flat on
its belly on an ice floe

a snake slithers

a snail crawls on its slimy trail

a frog leaps

a kangaroo
bounces

a sparrow skips

a grouper sways
when it swims

umbrella

a basilisk lizard
runs on water

fins

a water strider skates
on water

a jellyfish
propels itself
with its umbrella

a crab moves
sideways

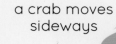

Feeding!

omnivores

the magpie's meal

snails

worms

seeds

the wild boar's meal

roots

worms

fruit

frogs

the bear's meal

fish

small mammals

berries

insects

herbivores

a moose eats aquatic plants

an elephant eats fruit, leaves and tree bark

a koala eats eucalyptus leaves

a panda eats bamboo shoots

a llama grazes on grass

a giraffe eats the high leaves of an acacia

drinking

a giraffe drinks with its legs spread out

an elephant uses its trunk

a sandgrouse moves water in its wings

a leopard brings its prey up in a tree

a hamster stuffs wheat and dandelions in its cheek pouches

a pika dries grass for the winter

a squirrel's stockpile

hazelnuts

acorns

pine cones

wolves hunt as a pack

moose

wolves

carnivores

polar bear

seal

buffalo

lionesses attack together

lionesses

whale

baleen

krill

an otter pursues a fish

osprey

talons

fish

Attacking and Defending

kings of camouflage

octopus

crab spider

giant guitarfish

leaf toad

chameleon

the "weapons"

horns

the oryx's horns

the rhinoceros's big horn

prickly ones

porcupinefish

long-spined urchin

giant armadillo

claws

grizzly bear

tusks

babirusa tusks

walrus tusks

elephant tusks

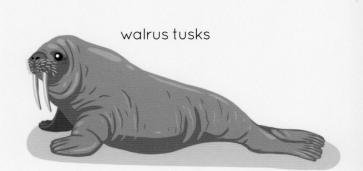

giant peacock moth

Indian cobra

frog with
eyespots

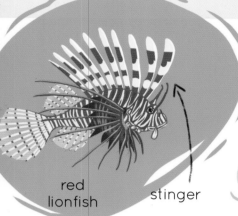

red
lionfish

stinger

venom

stinger

scorpion

alligator snapping turtle

scales

shell

a pangolin rolls itself into a ball

... and the tricks

skunk

bad odor

hoopoe

teeth

the jaws of the great
white shark

a tiger's fangs

the pointy teeth of
a piranha

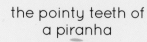

Communicating

calls

bees buzz

cats meow

dogs bark

toads croak

cows moo

snout

sheep bleat

hens cluck

zebras bark

elephants trumpet

mane

lions roar

bears growl

whales sing

hurler monkeys scream

wild boars grunt

tiger

mink

puma

crocodile

leopard

school of fish

pack of wolves

herd of reindeer

colony of ants

swans

albatrosses

gibbons

bald eagles

dik-dik

Sleepy Time!

little sleepers

a tree boa at rest

a dolphin sleeps with one eye open

a hawkfish rests with its eyes open

giraffes sleep standing up

unusual positions for sleeping

a baboon balancing on a branch

a polar bear with its bum in the air

a horse sleeps standing up

a pink flaming sleeps on one leg

big sleepers

koala

lion

owl monkey

little brown bat

sloth

den

provisions

dormouse

a long winter sleep

burrow

at the bottom of the water

brown bear

aquatic frog

marmot

a peaceful sleep

chimpanzees

nap

leopard

octopus

panda

hedgehog

comfortable beds

dead leaves

orangutan

otter

gorilla

leaves

branches

seaweed

Animals from the Past

flying reptiles

peteinosaurus

pterodactyl

eudimorphodon

quetzalcoatlus

dinosaurs

biggest

seismosaurus

diplodocus

long neck

pointy teeth

plates on the back

stegosaurus

tyrannosaurus

three horns

collar

most ferocious

triceratops

smallest

compsognathus

ankylosaurus

club-like tail

marine reptiles

enormous teeth

ichtyosaurus

liopleurodon

giant jawbone

elasmosaurus

plesiosaurus

long ribbon neck

52

diprotodon

mammoth

saber-toothed tiger

megatherium

cave bear

glyptodont

aurochs

tarpan

dodo

Tasmanian tiger

Unbelievable Outfits

stripes

coral snake

bumblebee

white tiger

okapi

emperor angelfish

baby tapir

red fox

fur

alpaca

Persian cat

hoopoe

northern hawk owl

feathers

peacock

spotted

giraffe

ocelot

stingray

leopard gecko

ladybug

guinea fowl

chinstrap penguin

black-and-white ruffed lemur

panda

magpie

dalmatian

shells

armadillo

Madagascar big-headed turtle

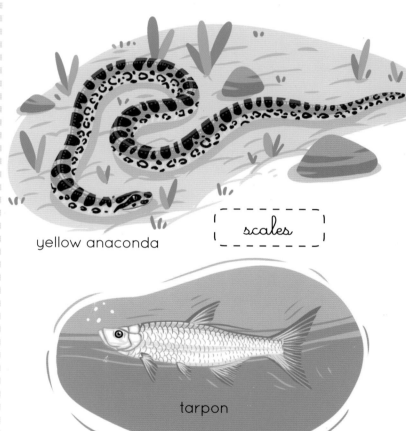

yellow anaconda

scales

Mexican hairless dog

naked

Sphynx cat

tarpon

multicolored

European roller

mandarin fish

mandrill

resplendent quetzal

peacock butterfly

harlequin poison frog

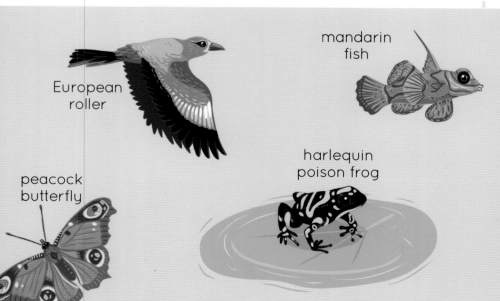

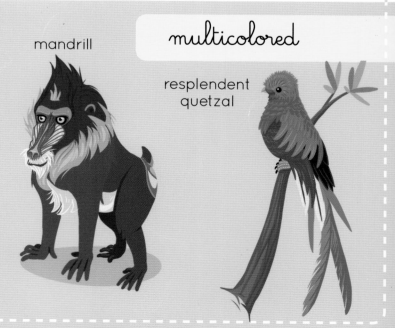

Record-Setting Animals

speed records on land

black mamba

ostrich

cheetah

the biggest

biggest marine mammal

blue whale

biggest fish

whale shark

tallest mammal

giraffe

biggest lizard

Komodo dragon

elephant

biggest terrestrial animal

biggest snake

anaconda

speed records in the air and sea

Indo-Pacific sailfish

magnificent frigatebird

killer whale

fastest fish

fastest seabird

fastest dive

peregrine falcon

fastest marine mammal

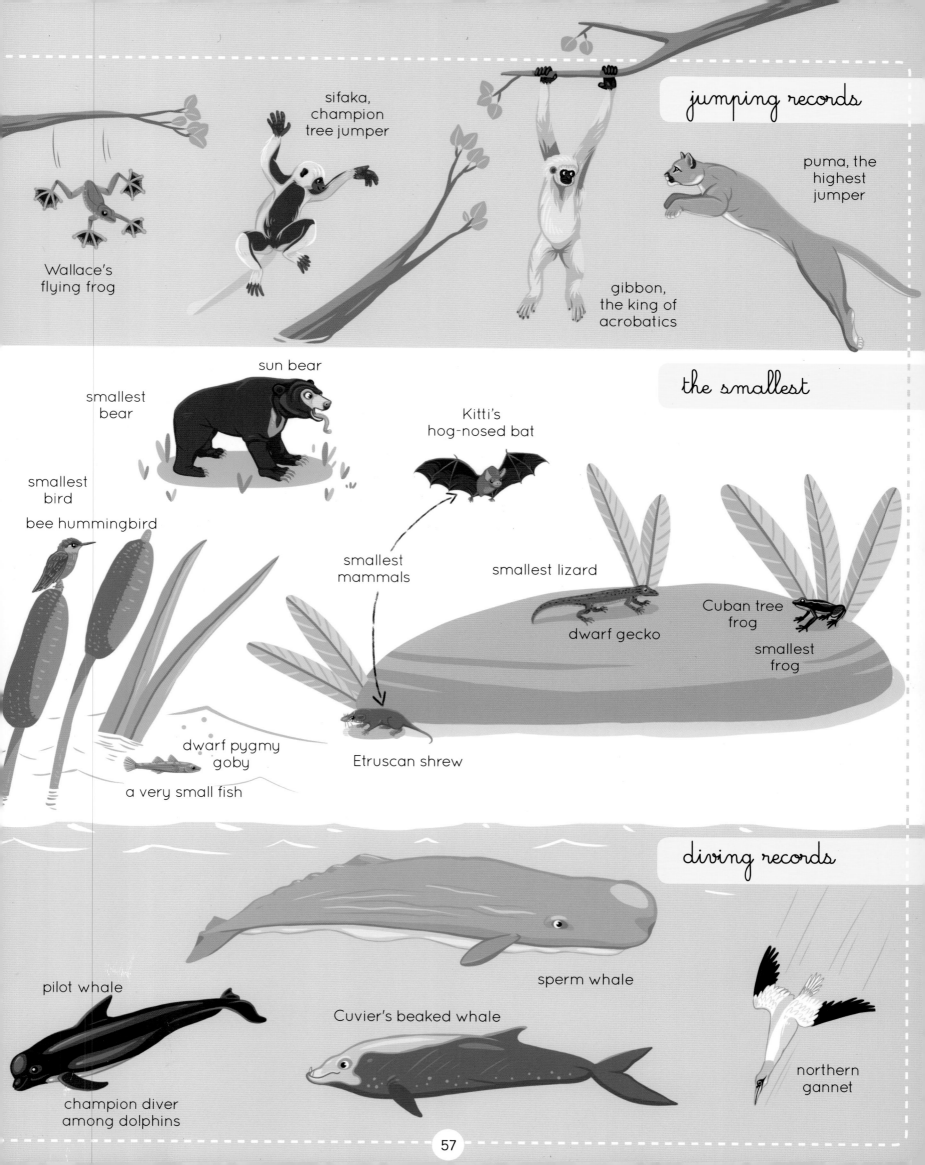

jumping records

sifaka, champion tree jumper

puma, the highest jumper

gibbon, the king of acrobatics

Wallace's flying frog

the smallest

sun bear

smallest bear

Kitti's hog-nosed bat

smallest bird

bee hummingbird

smallest mammals

smallest lizard

dwarf gecko

Cuban tree frog

smallest frog

Etruscan shrew

dwarf pygmy goby

a very small fish

diving records

pilot whale

sperm whale

Cuvier's beaked whale

northern gannet

champion diver among dolphins

57

Extraordinary Animals

funny noses

saiga antelope

snub-nosed monkey

star-nosed mole

long-beaked echidna

pig-nosed turtle

proboscis monkey

unusual aquatic animals

blobfish

Dumbo octopus

leafy seadragon

red-lipped batfish

yeti crab

sea pig

axolotl

funny heads

southern cassowary

hammerhead shark

aye-aye

emperor tamarin

uakari

mustache

shoebill

bush viper

goblin shark

scary ones

hatchetfish

giant frogfish

viperfish

purple
frog

hairy
frog

unusual animals on land

Cantor's giant
softshell turtle

Venezuelan
poodle moth

panda ant

naked mole rat

Pegasus

dragon

unicorn

imaginary animals

yeti

centaur

griffin

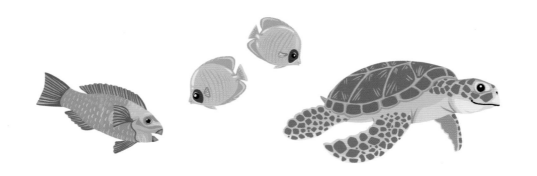